GW00724659

Martin Turner was born in 1948 and works as head of psychology at the Dyslexia Institute near London. He has published articles on child language, hypnotherapy, educational microcomputing and the teaching of reading, as well as translations, in collaboration with his wife and others, from the work of contemporary Persian poets.

MARTIN TURNER

———

Trespasses

faber and faber
LONDON · BOSTON

First published in 1992
by Faber and Faber Limited
3 Queen Square London WC1N 3AU

Photoset by Wilmaset Ltd, Birkenhead, Wirral
Printed in England by Clays Ltd, St Ives plc

All rights reserved

© Martin Turner 1992

Martin Turner is hereby identified as the author of
this work in accordance with Section 77 of the
Copyright, Designs and Patents Act 1988

*This book is sold subject to the condition that it
shall not, by way of trade or otherwise, be lent,
resold, hired out or otherwise circulated without
the publisher's prior consent in any form of
binding or cover other than that in which it is
published and without a similar condition including
this condition being imposed on the subsequent
purchaser*

A CIP record for this book
is available from the British Library

ISBN 0–571–16723–3

2 4 6 8 10 9 7 5 3 1

This book is for Demian, Toko, Marina and Tamsin

Contents

ACKNOWLEDGEMENTS

Grateful acknowledgement is due to the editors of *Ashes*, *Litmus*, *Sepia*, *Stride*, *Between the Lines*, *Poetry Durham*, *Poetry Business Anthology*, *Wasafiri*, *Other Poetry*, *Encounter*, *Kent Life*, *The Newsletter of the National Association of Gifted Children*, the *Poetry Book Society Anthology* and the *Priory Book of Contemporary Christian Poetry*, in whose pages these specimens, their ancestors or cousins, first appeared. 'Closedown' won first prize in the Kent Literature Festival national poetry competition in October 1988; other poems fared well in the Rymans New Writers Award, 1986, and the Wandsworth London Writers Competition, 1989.

The Meknes Bus

The blue panels of this old uncle
are flanked with dust,
tyres bald, every part careworn.
The day fades in the heat,
noise conserved to a murmur.

Without strife or clamour
the sure, work-stained men
climb the shaking steps.
One tenders to his wife
from a handkerchief of nuts.

At Asilah night falls.
From shutters and cracks
in the sun-bricked landscape
crowds toss through
the festive streets.
Fresh clothes cross the patient walls.

Cafés puddle the light.
Cradles of mint tea
still an uproar of flying hands.
Shadows assemble
to hedge or fight.

At Souk el Arba charcoal sparks
of a roadside kebab
spiral through the dark
where a tiny boy at his peril
leaps between spits to serve
one hunger, one meal.

Postwar

As the child listened, tears fluttered
at the edges of all the stories.
In aftermath his parents' war
crashed at his heels as he grew.

War closed around but could not hold him.
Always he would feel at home
in the regimens of prison,
hands resting on bamboo ribs.

He chose the fire-tortured log
that burned through stubbornly
in preference to wilting iron.
He would break, not bend.

Waiting until the white monkey
had died under the cigarette butts
of raucous guards, he buried it
tenderly in cool leaves.

His vow at the graveside
stiffened through the Last Post.
The tune — never-subsiding sobs —
he knew. But the words? Reaching towards

an Old Testament perseveration
they flared into evening radiance:
At the going down of the sun and in
the morning we will remember them.

In silence the din was sealed. The charge
of the earth ran through him but did not stay.
War left clean scars
but was all motive.

2

Newsprint begins where Dover ends.
It's what we've read about –
pottering in our ruts and lanes,
testing the weather (we have none).
For us no memories of mass
migrations and panning guns,
our dead never surrendered.
The sky, though hostile, rained
no camps or pyjama colonies
on our old homely soil.
Strain, strain and the lurid
enchantment of imminent death
lightened our daily habit
of blackout and our hobby, trouble.

Now all that's leaf-mould,
fallow and forgiving.
We rummage in a litter
of images unseeing
and hear only the lark-
cheer of an old tune.

Flags of Convenience

Nothing is interesting in my life except other people.
George Sand, letter to Flaubert, 18.9.1868

I

The conference programme is changing.
We keep tabs on handouts
and mix without labels.
The week begins to blaze.

At a certain moment of disintegration
the women take over,
warming the cockles of reluctant lovers,
then talking to each other.

The conversational order's past recall.
Unladen we leap in the cocktail circle.
Raillery lifts a surf of heads,
festooned with bubbles of laughter.

The second glass of wine ushers
away the work personae,
the flotsam of à la mode.
Everyone hails from Wigan.

I bob passive and can't fit a word.
Framed and measured, my looks good
but of a certain age, I seem
a lookalike for someone more powerful.

'Have you seen Harry?' The lecturess sweeps by,
and the lass with the aerobic conversation
finally tires at my confession of authorhood.
It sounds like another orphan.

2

We take ourselves seriously and collect the money.
By the fourth glass the veritas is heedless.
This woman glows and bounces
but work doesn't pay her bills,
it floods her single mind
in front of her students.

Now someone is insisting
on the articulation of his dilemma:
the transitory status
of educational ideas.
A bleak eye rises in the glass-stem.
Silence storms like the moon.
We yawn at our watches. Women walk away.
Unanswerable the question you cannot hold.

3

'The pupil–teacher interaction is multifaceted.'

The voice winds on its egregious way,
dinning the sanctuary of the inner ear
as, stiffness longing to succumb,
we meet again after the stern lecture.

Now in conversation the ground-rules are sufficient
for a swift début or re-entry.
So frail, like wisps of hair, we care
this tenderly for ourselves alone.

And we accumulate what can't be shared.
Children still tangling with one another
as friend or foe, dissolving in embrace,
diverge with every new experience.

The marks of age are individual.
Out in the bush the lion cubs grow apart.
They separate by tatters. Limp or scar,
torn ear — all aggregate identity.

Flags of convenience now fly above
the classroom weathers that have seasoned us,
each day alone enough
for our hard-pressed love.

In change the lure of equilibrium
secures the eye. But we're set rocking when,
from stink of nest and cloudy family anger,
like a figment a child springs, ripe with play.

4

We recross Queens
Mathematical Bridge.

On the lawns Bramleys rot
beyond the theorem.

Nasturtiums refuse
pearls of rain.

And I'm laurelled by a late echo:
'Hullo. Have you seen Harry?'

Patting

Please, no more patting of young heads.
The kids themselves don't exactly brighten
as you crouch in maudlin appeal, you,
a headmaster, and tell them not to be frightened

of *me*, the stranger in black.
This one squirms slowly and turns to a shy
dumpling under his freckles, ill at ease.
And what you said about *no tests* is, strictly, a lie.

At ten he can accept tolerance doses
of the truth without all this display
of jellified tenderness, the Portuguese man-of-war's
frilling of skirts in apologetic play.

If he were three and a half he might
have the sense to ignore this buzzing of words
and lean in encouragement upon the gleam
of good intent, hear the octaves and major thirds

in the spirit-raising chorale as you sink to your knees.
If he were five his patience would hold.
But at ten all this velvet has got him whipped.
Trust leaks away, the room turns cold,

and I have to unroll a carpet for his tongue,
clown, crow and complain till the air grows bright
with the clash of swords, his face pitched, body taut,
and sun streams in the room in lanes of light.

Water of Nevis

for Demian

Rocks or eggs – either way they're curled
around us. We repose in white
wooden spoons like Tom Thumbs.
Trouble, that boils in your nose,
subsides as you settle to consider
Aurelius' moral debts.
My tribute seeks the lace drapes
that pour, motionless, on the hillside.

All around us in little tents
souls are shattered by coincidence.
Songs would pump out their rings here,
their lyrics crying to be lived in,
and fantasy blossom like a dream-garden
with pink blooms the size of elms;
but the retina cannot resist
the etchings of a crisp lens.

It was my lunch – a gammon toastie –
you wanted, and not your own:
now you have usurped two
of my rock-niches and covet a third.
Such a long day thundering
after feats and curling for little talks.
The trees begin to blot or barb
the cliffs and sky of pale bone.

I reeled at the computer show,
brain aching with embedded blanks,
neurones and dendrites blinking
in hierarchies of control.
Menu-driven by levers
that thrill the hypothalamus,
to appetites I sacrificed
and for distractions gave thanks.

Here, it's true, the ancient music
rocks in its slow allemanic dance
more harmoniously away
from the trinkets of survival.
But at the cave of Lazarus
machines of high-intensive care
gather to see a miracle
emerge from pain and silence.

We've all consented to live among
strangers, calling nowhere home,
preying upon acceptance,
bearing unfamiliar names.
Elated and cast down we plunge
up mountains, sink into the ground.
Giddy with faith and fear our eyes
bleat of the hard way we have come.

Above us night gathers on
the big shoulders dusted with snow.
Water sings from end to end
of this cored valley.
We've negotiated, I suppose,
barbed wire, obstructions,
and worked hard to get this view.
To see the mountain you must stoop down low.

Colonies

I dream of you years after
you linked your arm in mine
in the glad late streets,
walking me safely home,
a eunuch from marital havoc.
You rehabilitated your sex
quite by nature.

Weak as kittens, newly born-again,
we were led always into a future
we never saw more than a day of.
And the word-of-mouth theology
failed its road test.

We ought not to deceive ourselves
with this colony more than any other,
free-floating beyond tradition
in its cushioned joys,
as the pains of staying
turn slowly procrustean.

The glowing eyelids and loosened tongues
turn gaga, harden towards children,
fossilizing fast as they gloat.
The lava is quick-setting.

Still, migrant through further colonies,
trustee of estrangement,
in truth I was too fierce.

Now I just want to lie beside you
in peace that would cleanse the things
that still grit in you
and pay tribute to your flow of hair.

But pigeons leak into the room
with poisonous bursts of dust.
They fly without hesitation to my hand.
I truss and stun them, swing
and toss them out in riddance.

Remorse charges me awake and into words.

Rathbone Market

for Ken Smith

Milk and blood pour
from these bodies that manoeuvre
purses and open bags
in the grip of wind,
our knuckles clubbing
at keys and change.
The city's cubes bear down
on our champion buggies
but the breath still flows
in raucous cries
that a carrot will appease.
Pain's a feast for some —
they harp on its *tempi*,
light at the spectacle
of its cobra dance.
We dote on what we've not got.

Two hearts for twenty!
cuts the market square
as we step back
treading among stars
in the delicate macadam.

Vine

for R v M

On the wind's pinions you skelter
through the trees, voluble dryad,
lightly or never setting foot to earth,
this quartz-glint of humour a far cry
from the rockery of malice or charm
in the common garden.

You who snorted at tropics
and frontiers found the paths of home
in the insect-laden dusk a fitter
maze for your padding feet,
the lacework of stars and taxis
an easier ending to bear.

And if the wind mumbles or tears
at your handkerchief or in stern
diapason numbs the roofless trees,
you can hedge your bets, explain that your blood
is a muddied cocktail
of orchid sunsets.

But now down in the mouth you tramp
acutely raging, though you keep
your rueful glitter as you scan,
visiting with an inquisitive glance
the spot where each man sits at peace
beneath a wreathing vine.

Old Men

Politics is a game for old men,
for grey beards, manacled hands,
chairs tilting in doorways.
The eloquent fingers run on,
or postpone a small match.
Water comes in an old kettle.

From the skin of the sea appear
its many moods: always
peaks of hardness ripen
into baffling compromise,
or melt at the tyranny
of too much definition.

The little tides slip by
in cycles that prove
nothing new can happen,
a long lesson that yields,
eventually, a weapon.
Even arguments have become

dense with solemnity, the quarrels
ceremonious as backgammon.
Young men rush on the sword.
Old men, sorrowing, clasp
mint tea, judge the true moment
to pitch their long-hoarded weight.

A small wind curls at the posters.
Quick-flowing souls are slowed
and changeable ones are set.
All the postures of would-be
are unleaved to show at last
the wizard in the cradle.

Look, the dynastic clouds
could be kites, bridled in such
sure hands that drop a confederate
kitten with equal cunning.
In the end there is time
for politics, always time.

The Master

In old age I comfort myself
with bits and pieces of food
and light, resisting extinction,
attentive to supply.

To the simple mind all is distortion.
Under my omniscient nose
the smell of a bad fact
is snuffed away, each scrap

of data patched to the quilt
of the world. You need me,
my decisively retorted formulae.
We clean up our concepts together.

In the swirl of influence the puppets kick
in sudden mannerism,
a slipstream of philosophers
plunging in mayhem.

Whence this apostolic transmission
of reverend cigars?
Great apes bequeath their habits,
radiant buttocks, even fleas.

Disciples? I abhor the term.
Each one comes to seem
a floating gravitational point.
I bode a permanent absence.

Nothing confines my view.
A favourite pupil, rising in hope
and catching for her breath,
dies in an interstellar eddy.

The Porous Garden

A rich tucket rises in the birds,
an ungovernable rush.
Overhead a courtship scuttles.
A thrush couches a hunting glare.
It was a mistake to lie embalmed
in an amour of explanations,
to think of all this as silent,
numbed by fast lanes, overruled
by majestic flight-paths.
Gnats dangle in the secret chill.
Tendrils linger in the small winds.
Shadows sculpt a tulip's sleep.

In contredanse neighbours parley
drinks as the tree's print
sharpens on the cropped lawn.
Birds fire their passing drills
and flirt with the sun in arch and crook.
An invalid in a shawl clings
thirstily to the tall sky.
Sun foments his upper skins.
One mind's dry forge churns on itself,
waiting, without power of event,
heeding smells of wet-brushed concrete.

Leaving a Home

Waking, the nightmare smacks against
a solid back garden wall
of sound raised by fruity birds.
Even worms tiptoe and sing.
I brush through the house,
through solid light and air,
still dreaming, shaking it all down,
to land in a clean kitchen.
The slide into expense, into
breaking up in rented rooms,
pensioning hot water with neighbours,
is broken with a fast.
Upstairs women cling to their sleep,
breath lifting smooth flanks,
true lineaments of a house.

Burial

for Mags Laver

The non-human, miscalled evil,
broods around mountains
that rise on every hand,
toys for the reaching,
or wreathed holy ground
that names us phantoms.

Aghast, you knelt beside
the door into the earth.
The crowd flowed to the wound,
a tableau vivant,
held on its hub, rotund.
Each one turned back alone.

Assigning all to good,
you peel the black sweater
you wore today only
because it was his,
relieved when a stricken child
begins to think of food.

Pioneer

The images touched you so gently you could die.
A cat's-cradle of family and fortune
allowed you to balance while you could.
With compass and set-square on the canvas
you brushed away the blur in your eye.

But then the marriage ran away screaming
to a flailing of thighs and need in a closed back room,
babies in quick succession in the duct,
another whispered pact
between chequebook and womb.

Still as glass you lay in the old
Edinburgh hospital whose windows
framed a decent emptiness for life.
And you made new drawings, tiny but pure,
tungsten instead of tarnished gold.

Soon the horizon fell away at your heels.
A capsule nosing at its own shock waves
carried earth's geometries towards a meld
of futures, all the proportions sure
of pristine man, seeds sown among equals.

Honey Double

Twins, and before I had begun to fathom
your arch *double entendres* I was fainting
in love with each of you in turn,
spun by Floyd Kramer's *On The Rebound*.

Puppyish, not old enough to know my way
through the fog of feminine seduction,
and merely mystified by the fancy
footsy under the table,

under your mother's grimly patient visage
I was more than half-willingly sucked in
to the whirlpools of helpless laughter
about the telephone switchboard.

Two wombs, two force-fields, honey double –
alas, my first centripetal petting
was still far off. Through your bathroom
keyhole I saw next to nothing.

In the safe box-room we sat at Risk
in the odour of friendship and body warmth.
Never rivals, together you explored
your schoolboy visitor's pubertal wits.

In the end it was each other you loved best.
But on Sorrel Point I still try and glean,
between raging tide and lacing wind
in the soft-branched heather, what oozing
cream buns you could possibly mean.

Three Poems from the Modern Persian of Sohrab Sepehri (1928–80)

translated with Farah Turner

NENUPHAR

(*Ipomoea Violacea:* 'heavenly blue morning-glory')

Past the frontiers of dream
the shadow of a nenuphar
had darkened some ruins.
What intrepid wind
had borne this nenuphar seed
to the place of my dreams?

Behind the dream's glass doors
and in the marsh-depths of mirrors,
wherever I had deadened
a corner of myself,
a nenuphar was growing.
Every moment it poured
into my emptiness
and in the din of its blooming
I could hear myself dying.

The veranda roof had crumbled
and nenuphar stems twined
all around the pillars.
What intrepid wind
had borne this nenuphar seed
to the place of my dreams?

It grew, the nenuphar,
rising from the depths
of my transparent sleep.
With the rush of dawn
my eyes opened on
my dream in ruins:
the nenuphar had twisted
all about my life.
I flowed in its veins.
It rooted in me.
What intrepid wind
had borne this nenuphar seed
to the place of my dreams?

WATER

We shouldn't dirty this water —
it supplies a distant pigeon,
a thrush dipping its wing
by a far thicket, a pitcher
filling in a village.

We shouldn't soil it as it flows
beside the white aspen
which relieves a gaping heart.
In it a *darveesh*
may have dipped his poor crust.

A beautiful woman
passes by the stream:
in the water the beauty
of her face is double!

Water and light in clear folds!
In the village upstream
live kind people.
May their cows pour milk,
their springs bubble!
I know without going there
that God's footsteps pass
close by their wattle huts.
Moonlight clarifies their expanse of talk.
Walls surely are low, low
in the other village
and its inhabitants know
the poppy's true value.
There water is water-blue!
A bud opens – they know it.
What a village it must be!
May the songs of evening hum
along their orchard paths!
Understanding the water
they live beside
they didn't dirty it
– nor should we.

OASIS IN A MOMENT

If you're coming to call on me,
I'm the far side of Oblivion,
somewhere beyond nowhere,
where pathways branch in the air
for travelling dandelion seeds
and news of the opening
of earth's farthest shrub.

On the sands are hoofprints
of graceful horsemen
who have ridden at dawn to climb
the hill of rising poppies.
Beyond Oblivion the umbrella
of desire is open:
as soon as thirst tingles
in a leaf stem the rain's
bell rings for refreshment.
And one is quite alone here.
As in a desert the elm's shadow
flows forward indefinitely.

If you're calling on me,
approach very gently
lest you crack the delicate
porcelain of my solitude.

Flyover

Neenaw in the canyons, in the fraught lanes,
as blood and vengeance vie past.
The splash of adrenalin on arterial walls
corrodes judgement.

Like a bar-chart the city
rises in panegyric,
shapes scissoring the wind,
glass glinting at the bezel.

Plants and posters
service the digestion.
From the Town Hall, level ten,
the view is all logic.

Everything is realized except the flaw.

Fatigue cowers in a fine
drizzle of phrases.
Wood frosts the face of concrete,
the lock of the forest.

Canteen Lesson

My grandfather set the stones in Blackfriars Bridge.
My grandmother brought his food in a cloth.
An injured uncle queued for dock work, lifted
back and forth on a door not to forfeit his place.

Father sustained the union cause through eight
years of blacklisting until, one night in the bare house,
while we children slept on mattresses in coats,
he made an end of everything.

Histories leave out the Stepney curfew
of the thirties, galloping night police swinging
long sticks at heads in doorways.
Yes, I manage the council electricians now,

wear suit and tie, stare past the hot food.
Lads these days are stuck into jobs
without proper training, too quickly
to care about work well done.

Churchill built camps in Essex while we watched
food convoys leave the dockside for Surrey.
This Maggie's got the bit between her teeth.
There'll be no holding her now.

Panto

Tonight I am a child, hating Christmas,
making my face roar,
walking the tightrope of happiness
under theatre lights,
as the tribe stamps its applause
and party-hats circulate.

Perform! Perform! urge the sudden,
pleading, loved faces
of these polished women,
as from cave to Purley semi
with pantomime brio
they flap at the hearth-flames their men feed,
conjuring feverfew at a pinch
to blast vacant fears
or grasping at heart's-ease,
rounding the glow of happiness
behind which the night soars.

Origins

1

The gracile travellers
sweep over the bare plains
with rival bobcat and jackal.
The trees wave them away.
They tag out like a necklace
to mesh with cruel eyeshot
the zigzagging gazelle.
All grudge the least shudder
to their equilibrium.

Words are for learning children.
The aunt with deft stumps
leaves off attacking a carcass
and rolls words together
as she slowly flakes a knife.

A footprint and some bones
are their negative.

2

Sure-fingered boys live
in trees or below trees
and from leaf-bedded dens
rob elders with stained fists.

Butting in sudden combat
in a dark classroom the disputed
details soon blur:
in this battle, or another,
was gathered the slow scar
that gained over the welter
of public circumstance,
of blood-rush and abandon,
victory's reckless edge.

In memory's kiln
the figure jars, hard-bitten,
standing alone.
A triumph edged with shame.

3

In time books accrue
around gaunt reported speech.
('"What am I doing here?"
asked Peter suddenly.')

The girl in the gilt hammock
freckles in September's sunny
zephyrs as she explores
the novelist's memory.
She retrieves herself, dripping,
as from a forest pool.

But nervous adults parse
hot water, power, roof,
desk-bound in suspense.
Will late fruits still fall
from the family tree?
Housework, homework, Sunday school –
aberrations of civility.
Culture is what you're used to.
Cartoons clatter in the next room.

At the Royal Society of Arts

Purse-mouthed, each speaker tidies
his words: the lectern draws,
under panels of madder and woad,
light, punctual applause.

Above, gods and heroes tumble
in the surf as Neptune's car,
bedded in flesh and ocean,
foments the demure uproar.

With ancient relish the master
has feather-brushed each dimple
and thigh, to be executed
by low-minded pupils.

Bacchus and Silenus cavort
on operatic pedalos,
an allegorical cabaret
of maritime heroes.

Around them, soft as daubs,
their women wait and sigh
to be pleasured and impregnated
by a tint of dying sky.

Whispers carry our public-
spirited talk across
the floor, making obvious
the dedication and hard work.

No dissenting eddies freckle
the tide of laudable enterprise.
But curiosity lifts
the dutiful eyes.

Grave portrait-heads stare down,
oppressed with the new grade
of wheat, compound interest
and the Baltic trade.

Milton Erickson and Aldous Huxley
in Santa Monica

The log-cabin bar-room and the King Kong welcome
are a picturesque legacy though every bit as devouring
as the LA drought, the allergenic ragweed
and the rattlesnakes of the Mojave desert
where the sierras step to the horizon
from the mariposa lilies at the roadside.

For Milton an invincible uphill climb
from paralysis and a relearning of all the tiny
movements of the ganglia of muscle and limb.
For Aldous a delta of detachment widening
from his mother's death and his older brother's,
with just some brushed gesso remaining in one eye.

In the zoo of postwar Hollywood there are means to laughter
in the blighted world: the fortune-teller's recoil
from the anonymous handwriting of Charlie Chaplin,
picnics with Krishnamurti and Anita Loos.
'Don't anybody in this gang know how to read?'
gruffed the Sheriff by the NO TRESPASSING sign.

Aldous in Deep Reflection can answer the mailman,
take a phone message and afterwards recall nothing.
He settles in his favourite chair, willing somnambule,
while Milton, the psychiatrist, notes the prodigious
memory that can recite a paragraph or tell
a page number after twenty-five years.

The voyagers bring with them a long haul of notebooks
for their two days of experimentation
in Santa Monica at mid-century,
annalists of consciousness, first cartographers
of the spider-zones of history, the blind wind-tunnels
that draw down the beanstalk of the new self.

Milton's confusing: 'Go deeper and deeper
into a trance until the depth is part and apart from you,
until what once was appears in impossible actuality,
challenging your memories and understandings.'
'Really, Milton, it's most extraordinarily interesting.
Your constant talking is frightfully distracting.'

In Aldous the tones of Surrey and Eton,
Balliol and Garsington begin to lengthen.
At the bottom of a ravine he finds a naked infant
who grows into himself, aged twenty-three.
Huxley aged fifty-two and Huxley aged twenty-three
simultaneously recognize each other.

And here the vestibule, the threshold of questions,
is the ontological crossing-point.
Which one is who and how can each know?
And Milton is sitting there on the edge of the ravine.
'Feel a need to establish contact with my voice.
All this will be available upon request.'

Time holds its shattered cliff of fragments
in an upright shoal, to keep from falling,
while the many thousand hours of inquiry dwindle
to a single point – which is lost, and found again,
then lost, until upon request the Brahmin
explorer's hologram is slowly released.

Next day volumes of notes are checked
and a joint book projected into the future.
A second strain of polio will soon
cripple Milton again, while bereavement waits
for Aldous, with cancer and a brushfire
which will clean up those notebooks in twenty minutes.

In the darkness of Aldous' Deep Reflection
the work is prepared, *prima materia* raw
for tortured rewriting, the government of form.
With a brushstroke Milton can green a life.
For Aldous, the leap into the crucible
frees ideas from the noise of circumstance.

Long after his last ascent of Squaw Peak,
Milton sends patients up there, or out to restaurants.
Most of each day he rests, and takes one glass of water.
His patients, anonymous, continue to walk
by the public ocean, or tell grass-blades apart,
breasting their event-horizon.

Anton Chekhov to Astrov

Well, my dear fellow, that's how it is.
We're like all the rest and like each other too.
Did you think, with your medicine and your trees,
you would be any different? Holy Russia herself
is a vast counterpane of forest and steppe
across which mythical armies of serfs, vassals,
a 'rabble of princes', *agents provocateurs*,
merchants, diehard bankers and herdsmen
toil and travail, gesticulating together
in the failing twilight, speaking their hearts.

Of course it can never happen. That's why the stage,
like an iron frame, will serve to hang
and stretch the canvas of a few moments
short of impossibility. They're here. A family,
a few acquaintances, hangers-on, retainers.
A couple recently arrived. There is
some sort of geomorphic shift, nothing so much
as a story, a drama; nothing more remarkable
than your day, or week, or mine. The couple leave.
Human forms remain what they were, mere bundles.

Fate, that we talked about so much, has been
the lightest of shadows, a mere wing-tip
brushing us all so that we hardly notice.
And what happens? A mirage of sighs goes up
to heaven, the vault of disappointments.
Our dreams – all the same, mind – lie in ruins,

our castles suddenly blur into the piles
of glamorous cumuli, to belong in mid-sky,
not to us after all. Once again we gather,
spent lives, in the pool of table-light.

Was this what you saw, lurking at the end
of your bleak forest-aisle, twinkling there,
ignis fatuus for the lost traveller?
I set candles here and there, not to mislead:
to warm stiff limbs, to hold a rolling eye.
It wasn't enough, I know. So difficult,
this orchestration of tension and presence,
suffering the re-emergence of hidden pains,
and all to chide a brisk audience.
Lulled, they manage some brittle laughs.

But when all's said and done, my dear Astrov,
vodka, not morphia, backstage will do
to celebrate our little triumph that nobody foresaw,
our mood that cannot be given a name,
our gesture that, though they have forgotten it,
nobody saw. We have turned back the corner
of the little curtain, the domestic veil.
Now they have nothing left to linger
over but the dreams that we placed there,
under the eyelids, like painted clouds.

The Old School

for Sig Prais

The Commander had gathered a few of us,
the best, the second best.

The reversing of *The Book of Psalms*
into a dactylic jigsaw
of Latin elegiac couplets
was set aside for Euclid's
Elements, a textbook in use
for eleven hundred years.

We watched as he drew out
the *demonstrandum*
and, splint by splint, puzzled
an ingenious scaffolding
until a cloud of bric-à-brac
surrounded the planetary orb.
At its heart lay the angle, ACD,
to be proved ninety degrees.

He perspired.
We were with him all the way.
It was arduous
but worth it.

Until a boy with pale grey eyes
politely raised his hand:
'Please Sir, couldn't you just join AD
and make ACD a right-angle?'
'Why?'
'It's the diameter.'

A weighty examination revealed
no flaw in this argument.
The sun which had never set
began in austere majesty
its slow decline into
imponderable eclipse.

Daniel

Bubbling with talk
and a fourteen-year-old's
anxious confidence,
you fend off the grim line
of your father's tight lip
and the advancing tide-mark of evidence
assembled by polite firemen
in your parents'
burned, pink bedroom.

With

1

It's true you connived
at the epic of your making,
the gums and elements worked free,
the grappling of odours,

and so now do not mind
the stained hand by your nose.
You notice nothing amiss,
no foreign graft or strain.

You are all-familiar with
the tonics and presses of love,
the weft of the music which you continue
to hear as you hear breathing.

I play in the old places – we all do.
And just now as your eyes rose,
open, in an arc to plant in mine,
I glimpsed their tennis-court grisaille
and a sweetpea wondering if it was a poppy
or a butterfly fending off sleep,
or both, in a high bloom of summer
that looped into itself.

And what was it we played, playing the moment,
on the far side of the court
where, a fugitive from Saul, David stood
in our acre paddock?
What false halcyon hung
overhead at noon?

Your eyes are the colour of river sand;
your sister's, avocado.
Steadily they pan,
awed by sleep – ours all are.

For you we place stone upon stone.
Each meal call or cry
for pyjamas upon the stair
is a finishing touch,
a rendering and dressing,
a gesture towards completion.

Heaven is a must of moments like these.

3

With. You just want to be with.

4

Whatever I most want to protect
you head for with unerring instinct.
Who wants toys
when you can have Daddy's glasses?

Learning your ways I touch the pink globe
that holds a harness bell,
tinkle it carefully
and lay it on the grass.
It is enough. Now you want it too.

The sign of value springs from crown to crown,
ubiquitous as butterflies.

5   RAIN ON ARRAN

The day is glittering down, melting the rose bulbs,
the rowan clusters, the torches of chestnut and ash key,
bloating the tall birch that in the morning
will step out more lemony.

It was autumn then, in Brodick, if a hedge elder
had pressed our hands with a black bouquet
more brackish, homelier than grapes, the umbels
crowns for gaunt rocks that looked away out to sea.

The rain on Arran has erased circumstance.
The short white cottages stood guard at lanes.
The ferries came and went. We clambered
stiles, five-bar gates, and shook from our roots
with sobs of laughter in the drenching rains.

Of the little guest-house I remember eagerly
only the wooden handrail, the overfurnished upstairs,
your mother snatching at a green apple in passing
with which to bait her breath,
the awkward bed to which I plucked her early.

Now Peruvian lily pods snap in the heat
and shoot their corns from broken barrels.
Bees still nuzzle the Michaelmas purple.
How she tricks the seeds from an old stalk
that stands in late bloom, hale and royal.

6   QUEEN CHARLOTTE'S MATERNITY HOSPITAL,
HAMMERSMITH

Haul them aboard by their night-strings.
Here more babies than ever before
make lusty or complicated beginnings.
No room for drama or ceremony:
a glide through time is the best
or only sure way to cope.
Work has pared away all but love
and love's instinct for distress.

Quick eyes above theatre masks
plead a ballet of ecstasy.
Teamwork is guided by orbit,
glances of pure survival.
Underneath are padded away
grim smiles, lost love,
mortal breast and thigh.
We switch from laugh to kindle.

I stand in green gumboots
with Canon and flash,
watch the tingling scalpel
and hold out for three hours.
Stretched tendon and vein
like white wires in a chicken wing
mark the edge of exhaustion.

Womb and suspect tubes
are held high for me to see
and with satisfaction pronounced sound.
She has often hungered
to tear out the troublesome lot
and feed them to cats and dogs.

Giblets decked on the stage.
I look on with nervous eye,
proprietorial, responsible.
Life holds one further mystery.

7

You just wanted to be *with*.

8

You hardly noticed your caesarean fall,
the peaceful hi-tech storm that tweaked you
and wrapped you, completed fruit,
in a yellow Victorian shawl,
outside your gray mother,
your eyes now yoked with hers.

Nineteen months later, still not far away,
you greet the dawn with whale-song
in rising, determined tribute,
and will not be quelled.
Brought nuzzling to pillow, your eyes chuckle fire,
baby we have baked in bed with us.

9

You lose interest in your share of apple,
your peeled quarter-boat.
It is mouth-furred and damp.
You offer it in trade but claim
my up-ended, gnawed core.

Half-way through hers your sister observes:
'In the pip there is a tree.'
She places one, shiny, in her palm
beside four others.

Sudden orchards are scattered
across a retina of sky.

The Plum is in her palanquin,
her palanquin, her palanquin,
the Plum is in her palanquin
upon the high plateau.

She is a sleepy Muffin,
worn out with mischief-making,
she is a sleepy Muffin,
upon the high plateau.

Upside down are her warm eyes,
watching me, warm eyes,
upside down are her warm eyes,
watching me go away.

Your Plug we searched for everywhere,
dummy-*koo*? dummy-*koo*?
your Plug we found eventually,
dummy-*koo*? dummy-*koo*?

Rusty's out and barking,
harpoo chi migeh? harpoo chi migeh?
Rusty's out and barking,
harpoo hup-hup.

And now it's time for sleeping,
lalacon, lalacon,
and now it's time for sleeping
and saying, *Shab bekhair!*

The Plum is in her palanquin,
curls blowing in her palanquin,
the Plum is in her palanquin,
upon the high plateau.

11

Where do you go to when you're asleep
and what do you smile about when you're there?
Late at night, as you voyage through eleven hours,
I startle at your balm where you've keeled over,
smart as a pear in the lamplight.
Happiness unfurrowed. I'm glad for you,
glad to see it settled like a spell
on a human face anywhere.

[51]

You've been a thriftless debtor to my loves
and run out much in riot from my stock.
Your days are all mischief now. Which escapade
gives you most pleasure as you feast in sleep?
The plunder of my Spanish soap?
The felt-tip mural on your shins?
Your dabbing at herb-cheese
in delicate imitation?

You have learned to wave at flies and aeroplanes.
How many bumps did you have today?
Your bathroom step travels with you,
portable toadstool for a dwarf,
and lets you do washing-up
and give unwanted kitchen help.
Foozool khanom, the *very spirit and extract*
of trouble, where will it end?

Now we are *with*. You went crossly down
in your cot but rose with a twinkle
to see I was still there,
at my book under the lamp.
Your anger eased with a sigh.
A greeting led to an idyll.
You forgive *and* forget
— it's better that way.

I have been a thriftless debtor to your loves
and run out much in riot from your stock.
Together we wade back
to a confluence of sources,
my daughter father of the man,
kind future on my shoulders,
kenning a further view,
taming dragons with grand indifference.

If happy, it's we who are odd.
The shock of my own soul is like
the steady shadow of my aeroplane:
geometry flowing on the fields below.
Our childhoods meet – a moment
of fruitfulness, balmy glow
under the lamp. Enough,
more than enough for now.

Some Farsi: *koo?*   where (is it)?
               harpoo chi migeh? what is the doggy saying?
               lalacon   sleep well (lullaby)
               shab bekhair   good night
               foozool khanom   madam busybody

thriftless debtor, spirit and extract, etc, from Dryden's *All For Love*.

[53]

Closedown

The houses snore back to back up this happy hill.
Each man ploughs his own furrow.
Each woman drops her blood in her own bowl.

Across graves of compost and greenhouse roofs
dogs bark the night into chaos,
a chorus of neighbourly spite.

Cash-urinals flower in the hollow street.
Near the motorway, several valleys off,
rectangles are manufacturing the night sky.

In a spine down the hill, in padded semis,
children are banked, their dreams burgeoning
in fractals of strange ink.

Do you hesitate, charmed by a square of colour?
Locked in dark cabinets
are the tunes of ancestors' bird-bone flutes.

Now the blind horizon of skin
is a pillow. These thoughts scheme
an afterlife on the lid of sleep.

Entrance

in memoriam Iain Buist 1950–87

Floating chiffon of powder-blue,
the cycles of woodsmoke mount no nearer
heaven but hang to scarf
the woodlands that sank.
Gulfs of air open to a vaunting bird's
star-like twitter on a last pole.

The fell wind that laid all those trees
our curiosity danced upon
returned a week later with an axe for you.
I rise in surprise as you enter.
We meet disabused of spurious excitement,
the adrenalin-drip of news.

The hills of your face, your green brow,
are contours of the permanent.
Beneath masks the rag-souls
always wore a formless look
impossible to face,
the steel of the living.

Our families continue to rehearse
on tiptoe the generational themes
of property and A-levels.
The children seem less absent
but the chorus duly takes hold.
They will not stumble.

Oblivion cultured like pearls.
No one can tell how much an eye sees.
One look razes the living.
The ghosts of old oaks
slip their moorings.
A noose settles in the air.

Glassy eyed I sit, finding you naturalized,
not yours but mine
the strangeness that will not be hid.
The terrible look that unbandaged Lazarus
still turns from its defiance
to create a debut.

The Ride Home

Already stiff-legged with excitement
you sponged the cycle seat.
It was no shock, that first flutter,
that first sight
of the unfathomable smile
of the magnanimous womb.
Umbrellas floated by
and faces you refrained from.
Clouds of generous
mock-orange and musk
settled the fuchsia's angry red.
Now on a sill at dusk
a toy globe illuminates
like a dreaming eye
immense virgin loneliness
private as the night sky.

Still Life

I use my own colour-coding to map out
the horoscope from my Sinclair Spectrum.
These are the quarters, these the trines.
I'll explain it all to you some time.

The sewage farm is where we used to go for herbs,
disused for twenty years. You could break your leg
down one of those trenches and never be heard.
Gypsies and glue-sniffers fly there now.

My son hunts dumped cars after dark.
He says you can't *do* anything during the day.
I pulled his hair the second night he was out.
But he grins and brings the conversation round again.

In one rotting car with the police bill on it
he put a tax disc of his own. Condemned,
he loves them. It was taken away like that,
the tax disc not *that* old.

He and Basil actually came to blows
at the hubcap and tyre among the beds.
The roses were for me. And a Judas-tree.
Basil himself doesn't know what he's got.

My friend said I was a disaster on wheels,
shouting at me for the least little thing.
He can't talk in a normal voice. With the key
in the ignition I know I've done something wrong.

My Allegro's steering wheel is *square*.
We'll tackle the body work this weekend.
I must stop going out with him.
Although I'm bad I'm not that bad.

It's late. Far off the shades of childhood
are rolling in great shames.
Home is through a brick-dark desert.
I can't explain the trines. There isn't time.

You Come to Me

You come to me suddenly
like a journalist in a small Italian town,
chuffed at voicing one of my
unspoken questions,
my unanswered, unspoken questions.

But there are many such
and at the first penetration of your voice
they flock into the air, a dark mob, crying:
'My God, it moves.
And we thought it was a church.'

A Blade of Light

in memoriam Samuel Beckett 1906–89

He is finished, he says. He has worn out
the years with his patience, this fisherman
or grey-green sailor I see.

Waiting is the better part of action, he says.
He has stood and stood. A hungry man,
he says, has no religion.

Sting of sea air. A log of oar
bumps in the shoals. A frame of a boat.
A littoral deserted, even when he's there.

A loaf of bread is harvested in a season
and nourishes
for just a week.

Wind at his temples like fingers on ivories.
The cuts of age have made
chines in his face, where the light fallows.

He sees no shoppers. He scans with empty eye.
He trains his ear
till it settles.

He has the litter of detail, but sees and hears
nothing while he follows a thought.
He cannot follow a thought very far.

He sees the crane-fly
in the giraffe, the kangaroo
in the Alsatian.

At the year's end he coils dry hands,
knowing midwinter
brings no halcyon.

The fish arrive like jewels in his net,
laundered from deep pasts.
He enters the waters of invisibility

like a blade of light.
He has finished. He turns
through the crowded beach and comes towards me.

Visitors

Poetry's won.   Holub

Your new editor's from the meat trade
and still keeps a cleaver on his wall.
His hopes aspire with yours, though quality
proves elusive in the circulation trawl.
You've still not got a quote, you complain, after two hours
of my talk in which you've written nothing at all.

You don't know what to write. You bask in my time.
Tribune of the fourth estate hobnobs with secular priest.
But those icebreaker photographs you brought, ceauçescu's
nearly aborted orphans, seem lifesize: the soul's at least
rock-like in those berry-eyes around which in the sun
deformed and flange limbs course, a photographer's feast.

It all adds to the moment of light, of company,
you didn't intend us to dwell upon.
Fresh teddy-bears lined back against the wall
may not be touched when donating visitors have gone.
Carts of wood fragments furnished with string
move on toy wheels across a metre or two of stone.

ceauçescu, ceauçescu, they've chopped off your capital.
Couldn't you see anything? Don't you have a plea of evil?
Calling us *C3s, honkies, donkeys, wasps*
or *Polish officer-class* was already hostile.
Katyn Wood, the bullet in the neck – Stalin's taste
was for the perfectly segmented customer-base.

So there's no victims' roulette, no sociological gamble,
after all, by which we stream into the dawn,
but a moral adventure in which we are all equal
and a particular one at that: a lesson learned
and forgotten daily upon the slave-trail
as pasty morning faces lift to shrill telephones.

Europe heaves in its coma; faces float to the light.
Flickering in the cell which has become universal,
a child's small life, its irritable fight
a light-signature on video, an after-ebb of movement.
Yes, in that vacuum poetry's won all right.
Here though it abhors the editorial.

'The magnolia laid its eggs on the ground.'
That is an observation I can offer you
free, as you gather your photographs
and thoughtless page and prepare to go.
And my 'dog-catchers and dealers in pitchblende'?
A story of any kind will do,

if in our English stupor we could agree
to continue, you with each column centimetre
and I with my purist poetry,
our elevation in spellbinding soap-opera,
rising through viscous reverie
to greet each detail like an avatar.

We paddle in some fond body, go shopping
for mini kabanos and wild mint soap
(just the bare necessities), everything
from a thermal bean bed for the Lhaso Apso
to a Blue Belton's collar with homing device ring.
Important games conjure the fires of hope.

This country is governed by an argument
audible as a dull concussion of blunders.
Every spite and qualm of heart is given vent
for the correspondent trained on tips and backhanders.
He rises from shark's-fin soup for his, and our, moment
as tourists and terrorists exchange their thunders.

In supermarket aisles, girls' winking beauty
catches cumbersome, fibrous men unawares: no greed
can survive all that domestic pampering.
Poems too are now rosettes or cream-cakes, instead
of the language of grown-ups overheard by children,
spurs to wide living, or spears to sainthood.

But still the children come, drawn by
welcome dread – trustful eavesdroppers –
to shrug off 'the end of history'
and settle on chair-arms like attentive dippers
to rehearse old endings, start the new journey
into transparency – jogged by malaise, like the shoppers.

Inexplicable frustrations seem to occur,
with shame, silence and the odd, tragic joke.
The hills, it turns out, and the coiling Thames down there
preserve the secret of good and bad luck
in the churchyard cot, in mournful sepia,
in the graceful silvering of whiskered folk.

In their brush with art those short-tailed burghers
became Carpeaux bronze the colour of drainpipe,
leaving to Soames Forsyte and others younger
substance and horse-sense to improve or keep,
before settling the details with notary or broker
and turning aside to a country churchyard to sleep.

But the effect fails, the children hear something else.
What they wrap away in tissue is not the heirloom.
And what, already beset with memories, they catch,
the lurch of kindness, soul made real at home,
surprises them, is not what they hoped for
at the point of hesitation in a crowded room.

But still the children come – our visitors,
whether with six earrings, shaved heads, underground
in sawn-off tee-shirts and eighteen-hole combat boots,
or as school clarinettists consorting for a round
of applause like jubilant pelicans, before silence
whitens the atoms of darkness all around.

To a Dreaming Friend

In sleep it weighs on us, that nugget
of folly stubborn to resist
the force that's irresistible.
By day though, beach kids that we are,

fearless of tides, as stubbornly
unable to cease patterning
bailey and barbican,
we raise stone upon subtle stone,

knowing that such smoothness
will not co-operate for long.
Tiles of eternity, they are
long since surrendered to their medium.

But still we try. It is our way.
Grief does not delay us. Why
such persistence? We can't even say
what we do. We try and try.

Platform Party

We ready ourselves. Tea and impeccable
public visors. Soon lift-off.
Mustered, we adjust our pleats and small,
paltering talk which soon palls.

These are the dry upper airs of power,
yet every corridor's a cul-de-sac
that does not lead to bed, the deep
genetic kitchen, one escape.

And these bowed, conferenced heads belong
to panting mammals. Tucked away
in each cerebellum, the pocket
of silence that hears the lone heartbeat,

the hard stations of the night.
Far off, mornings still dazzle
that left an ache: the sun's crown
of gorse, the wind suing,

brushing the sea with ink;
love's afterimage, a pineapple slice
of iris; again the wind,
saddling the boar-brown sea.

The waves break in the hall. The steps
are carpentered to success, the one
point of entry into the future
to which relying eyes go. I will rise,

rise to this occasion, and to others
like it. My heart flusters
all the time now, like a fish
trying to get out of a basket.

Letter to an Emigrant Friend

1

Dear Friend: I spring the vertigo of the past, I know.
There was so much you wanted me to see.
I follow your route through.

After your faint, leave-taking letter
I gross these long northern miles,
heavy with talk and old news.

Yorkshire's a russet burst. Seed-drills
have combed the hill's nape with young green.
There's spite in the air for winter corn.

Then the chorus of stacks, your *opéra bouffe*,
stands forth on a rising crest:
a glorious upward hurling of gases
into a sunscape of applause!

So that was it!

2

I've culled my database address list
for Christmas cards down to eighty-seven.
Still too many? I'm desolated.
The patch of kinship runs into outer
darkness after half a dozen nodes.

And friends are frailler:
I turn up at funerals unrecognized,
not what anyone thinks.
The clarity of a New Year call
soon clouds with promises.

Yet outside time and space
a batik of nerve-cells
joins us in hardy links.
The postman's knock, a phonecall, a dream
conspire in coincidence.

3

Ethics flower from the vagina these days.
Witness *Dallas* and the other gynaecological dramas
as children low in their sleep,
wind streaming their bodies into shape,
milky loins that shine in the dark.
A babe removed from the womb by knife
smells oven-misted, sweet-baked!

Teach pre-Romantic English poetry at Massey?
Sounds a doddle to me. Surely by quiet
Lake Taupo *A Marxist Analysis of Birdsong*
would venture the kindly light of day.
Course you might see Ron Robinson, the quiet American,
bags packed neat for the road, still there,
not missing Maine nor regretting Guernsey,
prosperously farming now or framing city lights
in glass stairwells with junction boxes;
and Australian John across the Tasman sea.

Here casino people shoot lavas of light,
eyeball pixels, throttle telephones,
sell the arse out of the pound while they can.
There's a lot of cash parked out there they say.
Black Friday, Black Monday, and in between
a gilt-edged weekend straining on the leash.
Every cloud has a sterling lining.
Money dies — and hits high noon next day.

Writing in this hazard of a life
is like putting on a shirt in a gale,
difficult though not actually impossible.
Can these words again travel between us
as easily as they did once before
we began to bump upon unknown hurdles,
looking in the teeth of a blunt wind
for the words Alexander's hoplites
missed when they pushed East:
eleutheria, *swoboda*, *uhuru* . . . ?

4

Whisky-flare of a mare's tail
in early sky.
A day is not too long.
Sunset goes hunting like a galleon.

Your voice is all you were.
Life goes better now.
I see Lucy crooked in an elbow,
hear her cuckooing.

If it weren't for children's slow-motion clocks,
better than the time-lapse
of poor memory's stills,
we'd surely not move at all.

We fan into a leaf-carpet for young steps.

5

The view falls below the horizon.
The industrial millipede
sinks and doesn't stir.
The sun has captured the ridge
and woven inklings of nightfall
into late craquelure.

With a light yawn we abrogate
all of a spy's omniscience,
our sacrificial peace-keeper
with dagger and paltry cloak.
Sand falls upon the eyes
till all enemies look alike.

As I drive I play
with axioms like knucklebones,
clearing a dead route
through motorway and city,
breasts jogging my memory
in the dazzling orange night.

No one is fully adult
in the secrets of the womb,
woman herself a braver
of that blazing rim.
Above and below us thrive
the forces of home.

One voice in the firmament,
a dark-working enzyme,
burns on the rawest silence.
I myself must listen
if others are to learn.
Grace is, not running out of time.

Trespasses

'You can't tell the truth *all* the time,'
she says, shaken momentarily by an inkling
of all the fissures conjured up by love.
'What is kindly meant, is not kindly said.'

Face glued to the window. Inside, all the reticence
of beachballs, binoculars, teabags: a man's modest
taproot to creation as he seeks to fold himself
in oblivion before his time.

A spy needs few keys – people always talk
about themselves. Lavender, for instance,
'needs moist, rich soil, not too near the sun'
(the lady visits her garden every morning).

Through the embrasure peeps a picket
from the land of colour, of sun a world away.
'A country of cheerless pasta – all chill,'
announces the visitor in a whisper.

A child frequently finds herself off-limits
in this way, looking up people's noses,
remembering mother's plump, shaved leg,
getting the point without all the traces of argument.

A sky of stormy pewter like the sea.
'Not a single normal placenta in Nova Huta.'
Really? So much lies hidden under a rainbow.
Numbers, like skies, go on forever.

So forgive us our trespasses, our daily bread,
as these transgressions are built, birdlike,
into ziggurats of fastidious ornament
which time does not dishevel,

landmarks by which the traveller reaches
into the interior, paying ever less heed
to thoughts of return, to summoning telegrams;
our truths, beloved of explorers.